BEHIND THE LAND OF LOST CONTENT

by
ZANDRA POWELL
Illustrated by the author

First Published 1993
by ELOT BOOKS
CATSLEY FARM
CORSCOMBE, DORCHESTER, DORSET DT2 0NR

Copyright © Zandra Powell 1993
All rights reserved

A catalogue record for this book is available from the British Library

ISBN 0 9521215 0 6

Printed by Creeds the Printers,
Broadoak, Bridport, Dorset. 0308 23411

For:

My Family —
and especially
Winston!

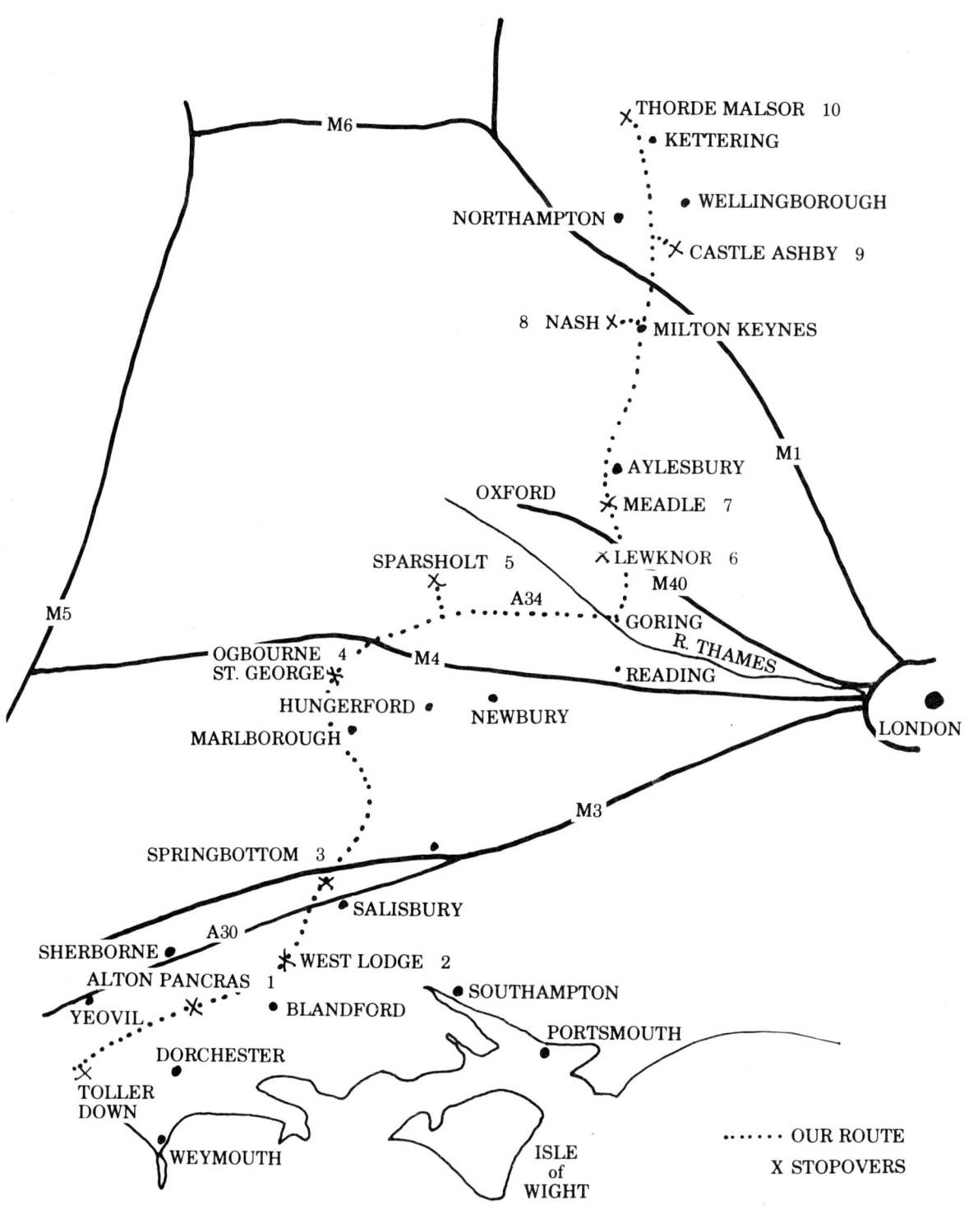

Prelude

"Who is sponsoring you?"

"What is it in aid of?"

"Why are you doing it?"

No-one is sponsoring us; it is in aid of nothing but our own enjoyment. As instigator of this expedition, I do not, as yet, know the answer to the last question.

Are we journeying to some far flung country — to one of the few remaining uncharted wildernesses? You could be forgiven for thinking so, from the weeks of planning, piles of maps and hoards of miscellaneous objects assembled. But look carefully — the maps, of course, hold the key to this expedition — the assembled objects endorse it.

Every Spring I migrate northwards from Dorset to my other home in the Midlands. This drive takes about four hours, depending on the number of road works. I have long held a wish to travel more peacefully, abandoning wheels in favour of horseback.

Not so very original after all: many thousands of people ride horses. But I think I can safely claim that we are the first to attempt to ride from Toller Down Gate, in West Dorset, to Thorpe Malsor, in Northamptonshire!

Four of us are setting out in May. Jennifer is the only one of my friends, who when approached with the idea, didn't hurriedly find something else to do. Winston is a dark brown gentleman, of mixed Welsh Cob and Thoroughbred parentage. He is human orientated; a thug and a misogynist with his own kind. Rose is a charming pink lady of stolid appearance and nature, and quite unworried by Winston's opinion of her. All four of us are middle aged and somewhat creaky in places.

Other people's horses retire to grass for their summer holidays. Winston and Rose range progressively further afield. As the heatwave in late April continues into May, our fitness programme becomes something of an ordeal. At slow paces, we are taking four hours to cover twelve miles; our longest planned days will be between thirty and forty miles.

The heatwave intensifies, and so do our misgivings. How tough will we all prove to be? Will our ride develop into a calling-on-hidden-depths character building marathon? It was intended as a gentle cross country ramble — and all our characters are long past the building stage. A change of tactics sees us riding at dawn: this is cool and pleasant, but will our hosts en route be happy about daybreak breakfasts?

Days before our departure, the heatwave breaks. The weather becomes cool and cloudy and more in keeping with our planned waterproofing. Tomorrow we will assemble here in our yard, and pack the horses at leisure. We have only seventeen miles to our first stop, and are not expected before drinks time. We plan to leave after a light lunch — all our organisation and saddlebag rehearsals put to orderly use!

Day One: Toller Down to Alton Pancras

I'm awake early, after a fragmented night's sleep, haunted by the feeling that I have forgotten to arrange accommodation somewhere.

Our first problem starts with a pre-breakfast telephone call:

"Something awful has happened!" Jennifer is noisy on the telephone. Visions of Rose with colic engulf me.

"It's the ceiling — Charlie has flooded the ceiling . . ."

I am trying to gather my still dopey senses; perhaps Rose is alright after all. It transpires that Jennifer's son has left a bathroom tap on overnight, and seven hours worth of water is floating around downstairs in the kitchen. She sounds slightly hysterical, and I make soothing noises and cross my fingers.

At midday, a somewhat sheepish Charlie arrives with piles of saddlebags stowed in the back of his mother's car. Minutes later, and Rose and Jennifer appear. We all studiously avoid the subject of taps and ceilings, and start to pack the horses. Much thought and pruning has gone into this exercise, but they do look rather bulky.

No matter. The last bag is strapped on; the map with our route carefully folded in a plastic bag is attached, and we are ready to leave.

"Horse, you are looking happy!" is Charlie's descriptive, if not entirely tactful comment, as he views his laden erstwhile hunter.

We mount with difficulty over our baggage, pose for photographs and are off at last!

As we leave the yard, one vital 'D' ring on my saddle snaps. This instantaneously upsets all my long planned packing arrangements, and I have to make emergency baler twine adjustments. No turning back now — J is coming to dinner at our first stop, and promises running repairs on arrival.

We clatter self-consciously down the road and into the first field. Winston and Rose break into a trot. Everything flaps and slips, and we accelerate and buck. As I'm still trying to cope with emergency repairs, I nearly fall off, and get the giggles. Three fields later, and we are helpless with hysterical laughter!

Feeling rather weak, we stand for a minute, looking back over the familiar views: north to Norwood and back towards Corscombe. Surely no views will compare with these for loveliness?

We join a small road from West Chelborough, ride up to Golden Cross, and after a mile, turn left down the track through Fortune's Wood Farm. This brings us out at the Police College in Chantmarle. Embryo policemen must be used to funny sights, as we get only a passing wave on our way through to Frome St. Quintin. Still on familiar ground, we climb up a track to cross the A37 Yeovil to Dorchester road. We had previously ridden this route, and so are able to follow the unmarked and sometimes obscure bridleways.

As we drop down on the chalk track to Up Sydling, a pair of hobbies curl over the hill close by. A few minutes later and Jennifer points: "Look out!" — and a buzzard flaps up out of the hedge at our feet, a snake dangling from his talons. He drops a few yards away in a field — a wonderful sighting.

Mallard fly up from the stream; this is the start of Sydling Water, tributary of the River Frome. We paddle in the ford to cool the horses and they drink thirstily. On again, and up over the next hill. The bridleway goes through a corn field; no reinstated path this, but evidence of usage. We dismount to descend to Up Cerne — the track is very flinty, and we are aware of the damage that flints can inflict on the horses' soles. I don't think Winston appreciates this thoughtfulness, as he pushes me up the backside and I slip on the steep chalk and flints!

Up Cerne seems a lost hamlet from another age. Unlike the rather yuppified house at Up Sydling, the old Manor house here, looks unchanged by the years. We see the lovely lakes on its northern side, as we leave the valley.

Now a short stretch of road, and on with the fluorescent green bootees for the first time. Surveys indicate these things to be the best protection against motorists for the horses, and we also wear arm bands. Quickly off the road and onto a track again, past the old Minterne granary. In the winter months I have delicious shooting lunches here, in exchange for beating with my dog.

We climb up Little Minterne Hill. The track passes through barley waving in the wind; Rose is convinced she sees a tiger lurking, and snorts and high-steps her way to the top!

We arrive at the bridleway crossing at Giant's Head, and find ourselves in a caravan site! The manager obligingly takes down an electric fence to let us through. "Never been used in twenty-five years," he says. Apparently riders join the bridleway a quarter of a mile further up; but we have spared ourselves the main road and followed the correct route.

Now, in open fields, our map reading is tested to the full. Both rather shaky in this exercise, we are surprised to find our way correctly for a further mile. We end up on a track which brings us down into a stable yard. Here, our host and hostess are waiting to greet us, for our first night's rest.

The horses have lovely accommodation: a roomy field shelter with two partitioned boxes. Clean water, soaked hay and mangers all ready. As an extra bonus, Winston and Rose take turns in enjoying an hour's grazing in the paddock, while we sort ourselves out and unpack. Cleaning tack is a necessary chore if we are to avoid problems, and numnahs and girths must be scrupulously clean.

Lying in my bath before dinner, I reflect that it has been an easy start. We have done a short mileage and no problems. Map reading, the horses' welfare, and crossing one range of hills after another, concentrates the mind wonderfully. All the problems we left behind are forgotten, and Jennifer hasn't mentioned the damaged ceiling since mid morning!

J. arrives for a delicious dinner. He does unorthodox but effective repairs to my saddle, and leaves, taking various unwanted bits and pieces home with him. No more motorised back-up from now on: we are on our own.

Day Two: Alton Pancras to West Lodge

The feeling of unreality from yesterday, vanishes with the stiffness that greets getting out of bed. A rookery behind the house drowns the dawn chorus, as I tiptoe creakily downstairs.

A hare jumps up on my entry to the paddock, and the horses call hungrily. Their feed has been dropped off or sent in advance to all our stopping places. It is a high energy coarse mix, and breakfast is greeted with enthusiasm. Rose's tail is festooned with shavings, but Winston has not laid down overnight.

Our hostess has provided a large and welcome breakfast to speed us on our way. Grooming and packing the horses takes time however — perhaps we'll speed up with experience!

Off again, and within a mile, we have missed a turning, and have to do a detour to find the correct bridleway. The horses feel fresh as we ride along the northern side of Church Hill, looking out over the Blackmore Vale.

We turn up through woods and emerge at the Dorsetshire Gap. Here, we sign the book, which is kept in a little box. Here, our proposed journey is recorded for all time.

The lovely grass track follows the top of downland with wonderful views. I long to stop and identify all the wild flowers: cowslips, early purple orchids and milkwort are easily recognised, but other treasures grow here. There is also a solitary man, just sitting and looking.

"Not too crowded!" he greets us.

Jennifer misjudges a gatepost, and badly rips one saddlebag. Inexpensive and showerproof, these were an experimental buy —obviously something more heavy duty would cope better. We must remember our horses are wider than usual!

It is obviously not going to be Jennifer's day; in Breach Wood, Rose goes knee deep into a bog. She emerges with clay covered legs, and a blob in her tail. Winston walks smugly round on dry ground.

We stop for a break, and eat squashed fly biscuits, taking it in turns to find somewhere to widdle, while the other holds the grazing horses. From here, we can see the wireless masts on Bulbarrow Hill.

We have a long pull up towards the top, pausing for gates and to look at the changing views. Near the summit, I think our map reading goes awry, as we climb alarmingly over rabbit holes, scrambling up near vertically over the ramparts of Rawlsbury Camp. Safely inside the battlements, the wind is keen and the view spectacular.

We go through a gate by a strange obelisk and out on to the road. Here, I imagine, was where Hardy's Tess drove her father's poor horse to death in its shafts. Here also, we meet a friend who drives past unexpectedly, and stops to wish us luck.

A mile or so of road, and we stop in a large grassy picnic area for our first lunch break. Refreshment consists of sips from our water bottles — mine a flask shaped whisky bottle and Jennifer's custom bought! Dried fruit and nuts is our fare, and carrots shared by all. Jennifer looses Rose to graze. I had previously read a book about a journey with two Camargue horses, and how their owners loosed them, confident they wouldn't stray in strange places. I have no such confidence in Winston's thoughts on the matter, and tentatively let go of his rope, keeping within grabbing distance. For ten minutes, he eats hungrily without moving, and I sit down and relax. When he moves, it is only a few paces away.

We follow a good track along the hill to Shillingstone. On either side, the contrast is marked, between the hedges and fields of the

Blackmore Vale on our left and the arable, hedgeless country, with large clumps of trees, on our right.

I am relieved to see, before we drop down from Oakford Hill, that the bridleway bridge over the River Stour is still there. When last viewed in February, the whole area was one vast lake. I had thought that this high narrow bridge would be our first obstacle, but both horses walk over quietly enough.

We forgot to remove our green bootees after Shillingstone, and discover at Hanford that Rose has shed one. Leaving Jennifer to hold the horses, I re-trace our steps on foot. Walking comes as a welcome relief to back and bottom, and I retrieve the missing boot.

At Hanford School, we are expected to tea. The horses have an admiring audience of little girls, and acquire suitable celebrity status. This sets us up for an unexpected hazard: a nasty piece of main road — less than a quarter of a mile, but bad corners and much traffic. One dilapidated yobbo-driven blue van decides to put everyone's lives at risk by shooting past us on the blindest corner.

With relief, we gain the safety of the Smugglers Lane. This lovely old track goes north-east for two miles, gently uphill and with soft going. Sadly many old beech trees have been devastated by the storms, but the track is well maintained and clear. We trot all the way up and walk on a small road to Stubhampton. Here a bridleway takes us along Stubhampton Bottom and into a huge wood — part of Cranborne Chase.

All four of us are feeling too tired to bother about the Gabbygammies — the wild spirits of the woods who haunt this area. Nevertheless, we break into a trot; the forestry tracks are good and we are running late. At last we come out into fields, and thence through the best bridleway gates I have used, to West Lodge and our second stopover.

The horses nibble grass in front of the stables, while we greet our hostess, unpack, wash and scrub. We soak hay and finally having fed the horses, carry our bags to the attractive house. Once King John's hunting lodge, it is beautifully sited; on a clear day the Isle of Wight is visible.

Feeling tired and dirty and out of place in such grandeur, hot baths soon restore morale, followed by a delicious dinner. Having dinner cooked for us each evening could just become a pleasant habit!

A check on the horses reveals Rose resting and Winston broken out in a sweat. I am instantly consumed with worry — has he eaten something poisonous en route? Is he in pain — or just tired, as Jennifer wisely suggests.

Our long suffering hostess lets me out of the house for another late night check. This time all appears well. Nevertheless, I lie awake worrying.

I have begun to understand the single-minded ruthlessness of people with goals. How dreadful if I let it override the welfare of the horses. Today we did twenty-one miles — tomorrow twenty-six. I hope the droves we follow will be grassy. The ground is very hard and both horses prefer soft going.

It will be a long day tomorrow. We must try and get a move on and cover two-thirds of the way by lunchtime. I think it will be better to do fast work in the morning and go slowly the latter part of the day. We trotted too much at the end of the day, today. I hope all will be well.

Day Three: West Lodge to Springbottom Farm

I am awake and worrying at dawn. Frustrated by the burglar alarm, I wait until I hear our hostess downstairs. At the stables both horses seem cheerful. Winston has obviously laid down, which is good, but he hasn't touched his hay. It unfortunately transpires that we soaked the wrong hay; Rose has chomped her way through it, but Winston prefers to wait for his breakfast.

We leave on a private route through lovely woods — very well managed with glades and plantations at different stages of growth. Our hostess comes with us, to show us the way, mounted on an enormously fat horse from the field. She points us in the direction of Ashmore, and we wave as she turns for home.

I should like to linger in Ashmore, but we must keep to our plans for the day. Time to notice as we pass, the pretty church gate, the war memorial and the large village pond. This is reputed to be fifteen feet deep, seven hundred feet above sea level and last ran dry in 1911.

Several ladies are waiting for a bus, and watch us curiously. Jennifer, outgoing and friendly, soon has them "ooohing and aaahing" when she explains our presence. They all wave us on our way with good wishes.

It occurs to me that however slowly one explores in a car, you do not see the intricate curve on a wrought iron gate, the lichen on a

stone memorial, and know the warmth of communication with those who belong in a place.

We leave Ashmore and follow a small road to Win Green, the highest point in south Wiltshire. On to the Downs, and here we join the first Ox Drove. This starts rather stony, and then turns into a lovely track where we can trot for miles. Some way along the Drove, we have to turn north. We dismount and walk down a track which leads into the Ebble Valley. At the bottom, we use Jennifer's old canvas bucket for the first time, as water in arable land troughs is suspect. We fill it with fresh water, and after a suspicious snort, both horses drink their fill.

We continue through Alvediston and on to West End and up a track to the second drove. This is the old Shaftesbury to Salisbury coach road, and hawthorn and cow parsley grow everywhere. We are intoxicated by clouds of blossom and warm smells — wonderful! We make very good time on this stretch, passing along the hill above the army badges, carved in the chalk of Fovant Down.

On open downland, we stop for lunch and both horses crop the old downland turf and graze loose around us, as we eat our fruit and nuts. Again, there are cowslips and milkwort, and trefoils and stonecrop are flowering, together with many other species. I wish again, that I had made room for my flower book in the saddlebag.

Lying back and listening to a skylark overhead, I am beginning to have an inkling of why I wanted to do this ride. Could it be that I have discovered what I hoped to find — an older, saner and more peaceful world, behind the noise and speed of ordinary life? I wonder if Jennifer feels the same way? We appear to be complementary companions — my effusion over views, flora and fauna, and celebration of all things green and beautiful, is tempered by a tacit "quite nice" from Jennifer. But she spends a long time writing in her diary each night!

More pressing needs interrupt my dreams. By this stage, we have lost all modesty, and widdle naturally in the open — it must enliven the routine flight of a passing helicopter!

Girths tightened and mounted again, we follow a grass track down the hill. We emerge suddenly from our peaceful world, on to the A30. This sudden transition is quite a shock, and I feel an illogical sense of resentfulness. Fortunately the road is wide, the traffic light and slow moving, and we cross the River Nadder safely, and escape on to a small road past the Green Dragon pub. Still somewhat intoxicated by our morning on the old droves and downland, we feel more at home on another bridleway.

This track leads up to a wonderful wood: Grovely Wood. Once under the canopy, we cross an old Roman avenue, lined with copper beeches. The sun streams through in shafts, and I can almost see the travellers of old, going from Old Sarum to the Mendips. We follow a track under ancient trees, with butterflies around the horses's ears, and chiff chaffs, willow warblers, blackcaps and a mistle thrush all singing.

Reluctantly, we drop down to civilisation again, and under a railway bridge into Wishford. The village shop is temptingly en route, and we make an unscheduled stop for ice creams, and to replenish our rather spartan lunchtime supplies. The horses draw a small group of admirers, and we pass the time of day, while slurping our ices. The village keeps to its history of Oakapple Day, when villagers reassert their rights to gather firewood from the forest. We read the carved plaque on the churchyard wall, recording the price of bread over a century.

Goodbye to more new friends and on to the main A36 for a bad crossing to join a grassy track leading up to more downland. There is a welcome abundance of hares up here, and several pairs of French partridges. How subtly the scene changes with each new range of hills we cross! The Dorset hills, now a distant memory, so different from the Wiltshire Downs, and now again a different feel to things. More arable, less bushes, different flowers — something that looks like a small lupin grows here. I feel as if we are on the edge of a vast plain — and, of course, we are.

We pass Druids Lodge, cross the A360 and on to a track to Normanton Down. Here we stop for a tea time graze, two miles short of our next destination. I feel a wave of euphoria at the sight of Stonehenge. So often I have hurtled past on the A303 and glanced sidewards at the tracks leading off into the green beyond. Now we have passed this way, and reached this far. It seems a tremendous milestone!

We ride quietly on, down the wide grass gallops, to Spring Bottom Farm. We are greeted by five star treatment and a lovely welcome. The horses, both dust allergic, approve their paper beds. I use shavings at home, but am impressed by the paper.

Another lovely bath and time to reflect. We got it right today — motoring on in the morning worked well. Long trots on the droves, followed by leading off the hills, good grazing periods and a quieter, slower afternoon. Time to spare for a tea-time graze and arriving cool with loosened girths. No sign of any breaking out this evening, although Rose's legs are up. Witch hazel and cold water bandages are the remedy in this knowledgeable yard, and our numnahs are whisked away to be washed in the machine!

Each evening we keep up to date with our own washing — bathrooms are festooned with bras, pants and socks! We have managed to impress all our friends by changing for dinner — carefully chosen skirts and blouses boost the morale no end!

Another delicious dinner, and so to bed — this time sharing the spare room — hope I don't snore! Hope Jennifer doesn't!

Perhaps tomorrow will be our bad day? It will certainly be the longest: thirty-seven miles. We plan a short cut off the Ridgeway at the end of the day. I hope this is wise; in theory, it should cut five miles, and we have checked that the Manton Down set up hasn't managed to close the bridleways. We will have our first 'Bed and Breakfast' stopover tomorrow night — I didn't much like the 'ambience' when I dropped off the feed. Rather active, noisy stables — I hope the horses will be able to rest — and bunk beds for us!

I'm also faintly worried about Salisbury Plain, and fall asleep with visions of missile wire, shell holes, firing ranges and parachutes drifting through my dreams!

Day Four:
Springbottom Farm to Ogbourne St. George

Fortunately our friends are early risers, and we are up and organised in good time. Before we leave, we watch Boris the foal and his mother turned out to grass; they do three circuits of the field, his spindly long legs matching her elegant strides. Amazing to think of someone on his back in three years' time!

We ride out up the lovely grass gallops towards Stonehenge. On the way, we pass a flock of guinea fowl in the middle of a field of spring corn, like a covey of wild partridges!

We cross the A303 by Stonehenge: soon this track will be festooned with razor wires to keep out the hippies. We reach Larkhill, where the roads are slippery and the grass close mown. Claiming tax payers' rights, we keep to the grass, leaving no footprints in the hard ground.

A dirt track takes us towards the firing range and red flags. As we approach, a large security guard halts us, inspects my letter from the Ministry of Defence in grim silence and motions us to wait. Is he going to check our credentials with Higher Authority, and waste precious time? Perhaps he thinks we are heavily disguised terrorists? He re-emerges from his hut — with a packet of polos for the horses!

Waving our thanks, we are on our way again, leaving the firing range behind us.

We cross the road to Durrington, where we take a few minutes off, to stand hock deep in the River Avon — a good tonic for the horses' legs.

Then we are on the training area, map reading our way towards the Old Marlborough Road. No parachutes are falling out of the sky, in the dropping zone, and we canter for a while, revelling in the grass and open spaces. Time thus gained is soon lost, as we pore together over the map, confused by contours and woods.

It seems we have mixed up the Wig and Ablington Furze — but — thank goodness, there is the water-tank land mark! We are on course after all. Very easy to go wrong here and add several miles to our journey. A compass would have been useful, always supposing that either of us could read it — which we can't!

We stop to celebrate with a 'Naafi' break, and are nearly caught with our pants down, by a convoy of armoured vehicles which appear suddenly in a swirl of dust! Apart from this small drama, Salisbury Plain is almost an anti-climax, with a singular lack of battle activity. To make up for this disappointment, we take a short cut on a tank track — and miss our bridleway crossing. A short stretch of road corrects this mistake, and we are up on to Everleigh Down. From the old barrows, we look back to where we crossed the training area. I revel in the wild open spaces of the plain, but Jennifer shudders at the bleakness.

The scene changes dramatically as we reach a belt of beech trees, and pick our way past a vast fallen storm victim. Fingers of beech stretch for over a mile down off Bruce Down, and we have our first view across the Pewsey Vale to the far distance where we will join the Ridgeway Path. We have a very long way to go.

The bridleway turns from soft beech mast, to a hard track with wide grass verges. Here we stop for our lunch break, confident enough now to lie flat out, eyes shut, while the horses graze loose.

We have our longest stretch of road through the Pewsey Vale — there are no bridleways. We knew this would be a slog, and we walk all the way. Rose and Winston have developed a slow amble, out of which they will not be hurried. A drowsy hour in the vale passes, without much traffic, and we reach a bridleway at last, climbing up to join the Ridgeway. New stiles and gates have just been installed here, and a farmer drives round to let us through a gateway the contractors have left unfinished. He tells us that he has seen three pairs of stone curlew and hen harriers on Salisbury Plain this spring. He calls us 'pioneers' and I feel important!

We follow a good track to East Kennet and trot for a while. Suddenly Winston treads on a flint, and is hopping lame — my greatest dread. I jump off and remove a large flint from his foot. Remounted gingerly, Winston is sound again, but bruising or puncture wounds won't show until tomorrow, and the incident casts a shadow.

We walk down to East Kennet and up the other side, past the Sanctuary, an ancient burial ground, and so on to the Ridgeway proper. This is a good grass track, but both horses are now feeling very tired and we stop for twenty minutes grazing break. We have reached decision point, and decide — I hope wisely — on our short cut.

Setting off again on springy old turf, we all feel much refreshed. We cross an immaculate gallop, the bridleway carefully segregated, and are suddenly in an astonishing valley! Bright green sheep-cropped grass surrounds acres of curious stones — Saracens stones — which give a moonscape impression. All of us are fascinated and re-energised by our surroundings, and trot on gaily down the valley.

Too late, we realise that we have managed to misread the contours. When we discover our mistake, we are hopelessly lost, and strike off in what we hope is the right direction, towards a track. Landmarks seem to bear little resemblance to the map, and to make matters worse, the gate I lean on to open into the track, is *live*! For a second, I think I have dislocated my elbow, until I notice electric wire touching the post. Winston, quite unaffected, grabs a mouthful of cow parsley.

Our elation turns rapidly to despair. We are exhausted and defeated. At the top of the track is a farmhouse, and I dismount stiffly, hoping to find someone who can direct us. I finally discover a nice man digging his garden, who re-orientates us. We have drifted a long way to the south, and he tries to explain how to get back on course.

Wearily, we retrace our steps, and get even more confused, as we near the Manton training establishment. Eventually we abandon map reading, and head towards the house. Past the fantastic covered exercise facilities, and we find an unexpected telephone box. We ring through to our Bed and Breakfast, to explain that although it is now six o'clock, we have at least another two hours to go.

As I replace the receiver, an important vehicle roars up, and we are confronted by our second security man of the day. Was it really only this morning that we had met our first? Instead of arresting us under suspicion of nobbling the possible  Derby winner, he is quite helpful. He re-routes us, and we follow his instructions until we are picked up by another employee — they must have close circuit television in this place!

Apparently two exhausted females pose no threat, and we are sent off again, down beside an all weather gallop.

We breathe a weary sigh of relief at finally extracting ourselves from this high powered nightmare, when Rose stumbles. Jennifer pulls a wedge shaped flint from her foot — it has gone clean through her protective pad. It must have pierced her sole, and the tip has probably broken off in her foot. What a place — and we never even saw a glimpse of a racehorse!

We decide to follow the road to Old Eagle, leading both horses. Here we pick up a byway on to the Downs again, and another decision looms. Either we go back to rejoin the Ridgeway — safe, but a long way; or trust that the marked but non-existent bridleway on our left, will materialise if we turn right. Rose seems sound; we choose the latter course, find a track, and descend thankfully to Ogbourne St. Andrew, leading the horses.

By now, we are all very tired indeed, but more cheerful. The horses walk with pricked ears, and we keep up our spirits by imagining the worse possible scenario at the Bed and Breakfast! A byway takes us to Ogbourne St. George, where we rejoin the Ridgeway, cross the main road, loop upwards to a Roman road, which leads us thankfully down to our stables.

Having expected the worst on arrival, we are pleasantly surprised. The stables have good deep beds, our hay is ready soaked, and in our little self-contained bunk room, supper is laid with two glasses of wine awaiting us! We settle the horses, and when they are comfortable, sit down at last to our own supper.

Too exhausted to clean tack, or mind about the dreaded shower, we fall into our bunks. I reckon this is journey's end, with two lame horses in the morning. J. rings, and I warn him to be ready to collect us.

I shan't sleep a wink in this bunk. I am too tired to be sad . .

Day Five: Ogbourne St. George to Sparsholt

I wake gradually, after a deep, untroubled sleep, and stare at the ceiling. It appears to be covered by something familiar, but in my drowsy state, I can't quite decide what. Of course! Rosettes — hundreds of them — how very original! This brings my brain slowly round to horses, and I'm instantly awake. Oh dear, today our ride has ended — I never really expected to get this far anyway: every day was an extra bonus.

The bunk above creaks. Suspense is killing me. I want to know the worst, and crawl out, pulling trousers over my nightie, emerging blinking into sunlight.

First I peer at Rose; she seems to be pointing one toe, which is bad, but not unusual in her case. Winston pricks his ears and burps, as I look over his door. I slip a headcollar on Rose, and lead her slowly out of the yard and on to the road. After a few paces, I urge her into a trot — miraculous — she trots up sound! This is too good to be true. Winston's turn next, and incredibly he too is sound: also rather cross and demanding breakfast. I feed them both with a light heart and bounce back to Jennifer.

"You're not going to believe this . . ." Her face appears out of bedclothes looking gloomy.

"They're alright — both sound!"

"Well, don't know what you were worried about . . ." and she turns over and goes back to sleep. I suppose it is only six o'clock!

No need to rush today — only a leisurely fifteen miles to cover. Yesterday we crossed three Ordnance Survey maps; it is satisfying to post them home to myself and lighten the load. We take a long time gathering ourselves together, grooming and packing, and leave in a laid-back fashion at mid-day.

The Ridgeway here is rutted, so it is lucky we are unhurried. We wander slowly up Liddington Hill and past the Iron Age fort at the top. Back to earth again as we descend. Here we have to cross the M4, and we gather our wits together and apply the green bootees. The horses are none too keen on the sensation of motorway traffic roaring underneath them in both directions. We regard this mass two-way migration with disdain, from the infinitely superior heights of horseback, and leave the world to its frenetic pursuits, as we regain the Ridgeway.

Lunch is long and leisurely. Occasional back-packers pass, all pleasant, and happy to pass the time of day. An Australian boy stops to talk; he has all the right ideas about how to see a country. No plans — just unrolls his bedroll as and when he pleases. "A bod's gotta do what a bod's gotta do," is his comment on the reasons for our ride, as he leaves us.

At this point, Winston decides that the best grass for miles around is to be found directly under Jennifer. Finding that heavy breathing in her ear fails to intimidate her, he puts his nose under her back, and shoves her bodily out of the way. I laugh right down in my stomach until it hurts!

We move gently on after lunch; the horses are full of grass and idle.

We pass by Wayland's Smithy, which sounds intriguing. Apparently it is a megalithic tomb, and if you leave your horse there with payment on the lintel stone, Wayland, the Saxon God of Smithies, will shoe it. We are unable to put this to the test, as foolishly, the gate to the monument is not designed for horses to pass through.

We are too lazy to divert from the hill top to view the famous Uffington White Horse. Beyond is Dragon Hill, where St. George is

alleged to have killed the Dragon, and below, is King Alfred's Blowing Stone, which I seem to remember visiting from school.

We stop again for tea, on a track off the Ridgeway, to avoid family parties of walkers. Rose takes exception to garish coloured backpacks, and prefers the company of the cows who lean over their fence and watch us with fascination.

Around five o'clock the back-packers seem to melt away and the Ridgeway is empty again. It has hardly been over populated considering it is a Saturday. We have a long detour down to Sparsholt, for our next stopover. This will be a disadvantage tomorrow, when we have another long day — thirty-five miles. Yesterday, we must have done over forty miles, thirty-seven of them scheduled.

Now we enter a very smart yard — or rather yards, belonging to friends of friends, who have kindly agreed to accommodate us. Winston will get an over-inflated opinion of himself if he stays here long!

Extra maintenance in the form of cold water bandages are applied, and Winston is lent some leg ease paste. Hard ground is taking its toll, and we need to press on tomorrow.

We are the first visitors in our hosts' brand new house, and sink deliciously into luxurious new carpets. The kitchen makes me green with envy, and yet again, we have a delicious dinner.

Day Six Sparsholt to Lewknor

Fortunately, in spite of all the newness, the burglar alarm is not operating as yet, and we both are able to get up early and get our own breakfast this Sunday morning. We are away by eight o'clock — and I am back again, on foot, at ten past, having forgotten the map! After this slight hiccup, we trot back up to the Ridgeway on good verges, one each side of the road.

Winston and Rose feel fresh, their legs are alright, and we have the Ridgeway to ourselves. A wide expanse of turf stretches for as far as we can see, and the horses settle into a slow, rhythmic mile-covering trot. We have our first view of Harwell Nuclear Power Station, a grey and distant landmark to the north-east. Hopefully, we shall see the other side of it by this evening. Up here, however, the world belongs to us and the skylarks, and anything else seems unreal and unimportant.

There is much evidence of ancient history, with another hill fort, and barrows. We pass the impressive monument erected in memory of Baron Wantage, by his dutiful wife. Grimms Ditch lies to our north, a series of prehistoric defensive dykes. Further on again, and we reach Scutchamer Knob, a Saxon barrow, where fairs used to be held.

The feeling of history is suddenly pervaded by a strange scene ahead. Weird and horrible masks are stuck up on stakes in the hedge. The track leads under some fir trees and into what appears to be a tinkers' encampment. Two dogs slink growling under a tatty

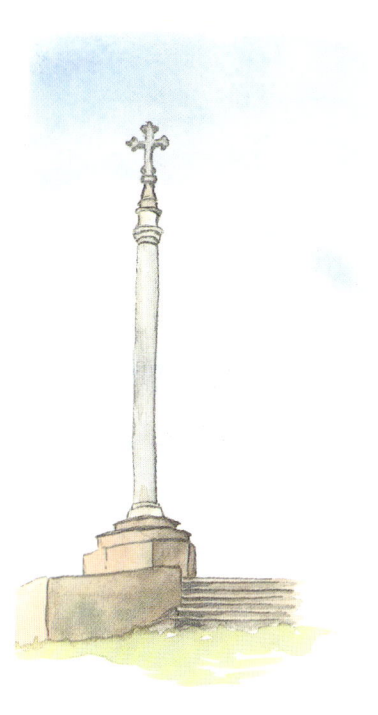

caravan, and although we see no-one, I'm sure a dirty curtain twitches inside. Jennifer and the horses are badly spooked by all this, and she won't let me stop and photograph the masks, convinced that we'll all be murdered! Now I shall never know if they are devil worshippers or part of some strange sinister cult!

I shiver too, glad to emerge from the dark trees and into sunlight again. Racehorse gallops are as numerous as old barrows and ditches up here. The turf looks wonderfully tempting, but the Ridgeway grass is also good, and we make good time.

A stand-pipe and tap provide an excuse for a break. Jennifer keeps some of her belongings in the canvas bucket, which makes watering a lengthy procedure. The horses shouldn't eat while they have more trotting ahead, and I skin my fingers on Winston's hogged mane, when he argues this point. At last the bucket is extracted and presented full of clean water. Needless to say, neither horse is thirsty, and Jennifer laboriously re-packs again.

I remember noticing a sign for the Ridgeway, while driving on the A34 from Newbury to Oxford. Now we pass safely underneath, cocooned in our slower world, as traffic roars overhead. On the far side, we stop to read a memorial stone, erected in memory of a soldier killed in an armoured car accident on this spot, many years ago. The wars for which he was in training, have resulted in the peace we have now. I have a feeling, up here in the wind and the sun, that his accident was not of spent value.

More gallops lie ahead, and this time, some activity. Something about the horses seems unfamiliar; as we trot closer, we realise why. These are Arab horses, training for the increasingly popular Arab racing. Although the English thoroughbred traces back to the Darley Arabian and the Godolphin Arabian, it seems to have evolved into a very different animal from these fiery little horses.

Beyond the gallops, and we stop for a 'Naafi' break. Bridles off, girths loose, and I lie back idly in the grass, while Winston munches. Suddenly I hear it — that most magic of sounds! Can it really be — here, in this setting? Again, the unmistakeable call of a curlew! I am flooded by feelings of Scotland, transported to wild moors and mountains — so different from this gently downland! The fleeting image of a dream passes through my mind — if Dorset to the Midlands turns out to be possible on horseback, what might the future hold?

Two walkers appear and bring me down to earth. Now the Ridgeway is becoming populated; more backpackers pass, and we are all at once overwhelmed by a Ramblers' Club — all forty-eight of them! Some greet us cheerily enough, but I am left wondering, as the last one passes, what pleasure can be gained from walking in a herd?

A voluntary code exists, by which motorbikes and four wheel vehicles desist from using the Ridgeway at weekends. Only a few red-faced bicyclists in skin-tight black nylon Bermuda shorts puff past — each to his own enjoyment — and it doesn't look very enjoyable to me!

We had planned to lead the horses off the Ridgeway, down towards Streatley, but at this point, several members of a local riding stable join us. Rose and Winston decide that this is hunting, and come instantly to life, so we remain mounted and ride along with the others, as far as their yard. They kindly let us fill our water bucket, which this time is accepted, and wish us a safe passage over the Thames.

I don't think they envisaged us crossing the river in Goring, but this is the direction we turn, when we reach the main road. All at once, we have plunged ourselves into a very different world. I had planned to ask someone to photograph us in the middle of the bridge, with the cascading Thames behind. The level of traffic is too high, however, and none of it has much respect for our mode of transport, so we do not linger. Leaving Jennifer holding the horses in a quiet side road, I go back on foot to a cafe we have just passed. Both of us are suddenly very hungry, and I buy a Cornish pasty for Jennifer and a huge salad roll for myself. Surrounded by smart tourists, I feel — and probably smell — somewhat out of place! Lunch today is a different affair, munching on the move down a residential area, in search of the first Swan sign.

Here we plan to join the Swan's Way, a long distance ride opened up three years ago, by courtesy of the Countryside Commission, the Thames and Chilters Tourist Board and the local councils. I believe it was the vision of an anonymous lady rider, and I salute such an inspired project. Hopefully it will lead us northwards for the next sixty-five miles, to Salcey Forest in Northamptonshire.

Now though, we find ourselves in quite a different setting to previous days. We take a little time to adjust to the riverside path, with smart white launches on our left, and upmarket, yuppy villas on our right. I don't think I would like to live here, because behind the

houses, runs a railway line. This, it soon becomes apparent, is very busy, and trains pass both ways at frequent intervals. What a contrast to the quiet hills we have left behind us! The horses take all this in their stride; they really are becoming old campaigners now, and are resigned to being surprised by nothing!

Beyond South Stoke village, where we leave the river, is one of Brunel's finest railway bridges. Apparently it is visited by engineers from all over the world. We make a dash under the railway between trains, and in our relief, turn off on a wrong track. This leads to a lane with good grazing, so we stop for a time so the horses can have lunch.

Retracing our steps after some serious map reading, we follow the road until turning off on the correct route.

Here we find ourselves in a flat and dreary piece of arable country. A stone track takes us in a straight line through an area where the natural way of life has long been defeated. Someone has planted a few scrubby little oak trees and surrounded them with wire, but they are surely doomed by the sprays which have removed all weeds and flowers. Only a large black shuttered barn breaks the monotony, as we plod wearily past.

We have ridden through such wonderful country up to now. We know we are spoilt for views in West Dorset, and are resigned to less attractive routes from now on, in this part of the world which is foreign to both of us. But I do hope that it will not all be like this lifeless plain. At the end of the track, we see, to our horror, that the metal gate is padlocked. Thankfully, at right-angles to the post, is a gap for the bridleway — a useful idea in a stockless area.

Over the main road, and the Swan logo leads us up into a pleasant lane bounded by hedges. Our spirits rise with the green surroundings. We are now on a bridleway which follows the route of the old Icknield Way. This lasts for some time, and then we follow a headland of a field adjoining a road, which deteriorates into more road. A council tip and a gravel quarry follow, and seeing the huge number of heavy lorries parked, we are thankful that it is Sunday.

We decide, at this point, to stay on a further stretch of road, rather than follow the bridleway round three sides of a square. At last we reach beech woods at the foothills of the Chilterns. Tempting logs and jumps indicate much equine activity here, but tired horses and loaded saddlebags are not conducive to 'lepping'. The track continues through the wood, and into open country, crossing various small roads and lanes. Winston stops suddenly to stare at a donkey — he doesn't seem to have outgrown his horror of this species!

We reach our turning off to Lewknor, just short of the M40. A small road takes us to the village and a quarter of a mile beyond, we find our next bed and breakfast.

Arrangements here had been hard to pin down, and now our worst fears are realised. The horses have a choice between an enormous field of lush grass, which would render them both immovable by morning, or a very poor tumble-down building with a broken manger, musty straw and nails sticking out everywhere.

We settle for adjoining yards as the best option, and I start wearily clearing away potential hazards. Jennifer soaks hay, rubs the horses down, applies cold water bandages and organises water. The farm owners are absent, but the bed and breakfast couple from over the road appear and are apologetic about the horse accommodation. They are kind and offer to help and carry all our equipment to their house. Rattled and disorganised, I get Winston's and my hairbrushes mixed up, but I don't suppose either of us will mind very much at this stage!

Leaving the horses with their feeds, and hoping that it doesn't rain, we go and inspect our own quarters. We have fared much better, and have a comfortable room and a bath at our disposal. We are having supper at the local pub, and decide to forego a bath until later. As our only transport is now resting, we set off on foot for sustenance. A glass of wine and a large plate of fish and chips later, and we feel more cheerful. Jennifer gathers an admiring crowd, as she describes our travels, and I discover that we are sitting next to three keen birdwatchers. They confirm that my curlew was not an illusion.

Much restored, we walk back and check the horses. They seem quite happy, although I'm worried they have nowhere to lie down. Luckily, we have our shortest day tomorrow and can make it up to them for their uncomfortable night.

As far as I'm concerned, strange beds no longer worry me. A welcome bath — under the duvet and I remember no more.

Day Seven:
Lewknor to Meadle

I'm up early this morning, although we have a 'laid-back' day of us. The horses look rather cold in their enclosures, but otherwise alright, and their legs are down.

Although it is only six o'clock, two other pony owners are already tending to their animals. I wonder what livery fees they have to pay, in this sort of establishment? A friendly lorry driver keeps a pony here for his daughter. He admits he is ignorant on all things horsey, and is keen to learn. I get the impression however, that he is considerably more knowledgeable than many horse owners who profess to be experienced!

A rather startling girl, with a punk hair-do and earrings in strange places, comes over to talk. She is very nice and friendly, and owns an Arab Welsh cross. She works in a supermarket and her money goes to keep the horse in superb condition. I feel rather humble that I come from a privileged background where keeping horses is so easy. How honoured I am to meet these people; how lovely that horses should touch so many diverse lives.

Deep in thought, I return to the house and find Jennifer and a large breakfast. Afterwards, we walk back to the village, buy postcards, and send off more maps at the Post Office.

It seems to take us far longer to pack up on days when we have only a short mileage to cover. Today is our shortest day — just nine miles.

We ride under the M40 on a wide green track, and meet a local rider who stops to chat. Shortly afterwards we pass a point-to-point course, attractively laid out in the foothills and surrounded by woodland. Hoof beats coming up fast behind us, materialise into a girl on an eventer, who has heard about us from the previous rider, and wants to know more! She leaves us to ride up through the woods, and we are tempted to follow. We keep to our track however, and pass vast chalk pits on either side, before reaching Bledlow.

There are some lovely old houses here and we wander slowly through the village. On the far side, a ford is shown on the map; it is not quite like that when we find the stream, but we succeed in clambering down the bank and tie the horses up, knee deep in running water, for half an hour of leg tonic. This idyllic scene comes to an abrupt end, when a muntjak deer suddenly pops up on the bank. Both horses are horrified and have to be hurriedly rescued!

They bounce down the lane indignantly and are still aerated when we stop for lunch. Fortunately we are in a stretch of grassy lane with a hunting gate at one end. As a precaution, we string some baler twine across the other, before turning them loose. We have the rest of the day to cover a couple of miles, and relaxing is planned for the afternoon.

Lying on my back, warm sun on my face, I watch through half closed eyes as a small aeroplane drones lazily overhead. Long grasses cushion my back and a skylark sings somewhere in the blue.

I am filled with a feel of someone else having lain here before — of summer days, of warmth and laughter. I seem to hear the creak of wagon wheels and harness jingling faintly on the breeze, and all around the smell of sweet, dry meadow hay in the making. I open one eye and only the horses and ourselves are in the lane. But, at the further corner of the recently cut silage field adjoining, a large green tractor appears, and starts to scatter fertiliser — and my fancies.

Our peaceful rest disturbed, we climb reluctantly to our feet and re-pack the horses. The bridleway continues through a wood and around corn fields with headlands left for riders.

We have time to turn aside and inspect Ilmer village. There is evidence of much care here; very pretty, but a bit too manicured — and a very upmarket car passes unnecessarily fast on the dead-end lane. Why is he in such a hurry to go nowhere? The church is open and we take it in turns to explore inside. It has an unusual shingle spire, recently restored, and traces of Norman architecture remain.

We wander back on to our bridleway and discover a burnt out car half blocking the lane. A bemused policeman is inspecting its interior, and tells us that it is a dumped, stolen vehicle. He has come down the narrow lane in his van and we reckon he will get a crick in his neck reversing back up again, with no turning place for over a mile!

Our next bed and breakfast couldn't be a greater contrast to last night. We have a tenuous connection with our landlady: she is a relation of a friend, and is looking out for us. She has a large, clean yard with nice boxes and everything is immaculate. We settle the horses and stow our kit in the back of her pick-up. Her bungalow is the other side of her field, but it is easier to take the luggage round by road.

We have tea and home-made cake — a great luxury — and lovely comfortable, separate bedrooms. We are shown round the large garden and admire our hostess's flowers and vegetables. Paddocks are divided by neatly trimmed hedges —and all the work done, with no help, by someone of an age more suited to knitting!

We clean our tack in the spotless saddleroom, and finish chores in time for a delicious dinner. We make an effort here, and wear our skirts again, although there is now an all pervading smell of horse around our clothes, I think! Some soaps seem to blend with and enhance this smell. I am reminded of my son, who used to spend the duration of Pony Club Camp sleeping in his jodhpurs and boots, as it was less trouble!

Tonight I fall happily into bed and blissfully into oblivion . . .

Day Eight:
Meadle to Nash

We awake surrounded by hounds! The local kennels are a mile away and summer hound exercise seems to start early up here. Two hunt servants on bicycles don't appear to be much in control, as hounds gallop all over the garden, hotly and furiously pursued by the owner's border terrier.

Winston and Rose have obviously not woken in time for all the disturbance, and greet their breakfast sleepily.

After an earlier than planned start, we have an efficient getaway, and even manage to leave clean stables behind us! We pass the kennels, and further on, a lone hound who is busily doing his own thing. A green lane leads into fields that are very rough; clay baked hard and potted. This is not good news — we have twenty-five miles to cover today, and can only pick our way slowly and gingerly.

Fortunately we are soon on old pasture meadows, which surround the deserted mediaeval village of Moreton. We have a stretch of road through Stone, and then we are within the grounds of Eythrope Park. This is an attractive place, with hump-back bridges over the River Thame and carriers. The Swan's Way goes along the avenue, past imposing entrance gates and climbs gently up over Waddesdon Hill.

On the top, we pause to look around. Aylesbury lies to the east of us and Waddesdon Manor sits importantly on a hill to our left. The house, now managed by the National Trust, is built in the French Chateau style, and looks out across fine views.

We cross the site of an old Roman Road — once Akeman Street, before we reach the main A41 road, by a lodge — also very French in architecture. Here we follow a minor road, but there are good verges to ride on.

Soon we turn off through fields, past Denham Lodge, a beautiful early seventeenth century house. Again, in this district, there is much evidence of mediaeval settlements.

We see two riders walking ahead, and soon catch up. This time, Jennifer launches into an explanation of our expedition, before the usual questions. However, we are met with disinterest and blank stares. Oh dear, maybe we are becoming a couple of old bores! After riding some way together in disconcerting silence, we finally tumble to the fact that our companions are non-English speaking Danish girls! From what we can gather, they are riding Danish Warmbloods, and are over here to study dressage. Neither Winston nor Rose have a very high opinion of dressage, and when our ways part, we wave, but there are no whinnied farewells — perhaps there is an equine language difficulty as well!

We climb up Quainton Hill and stop for a mid-morning break. Looking back over the gate we have just come through, the Vale of Aylesbury lies to the south. Somehow I hadn't expected such loveliness here — another part of England spread at our feet — beautiful and green, stretching back to the misty blue of the Chilterns.

On the move again and we climb over the top of Quainton Hill and yet another panorama lies ahead. More signs of modern 'civilisation' this side — and tomorrow we will pass through some strange places somewhere to the north out there!

We ride down past Fulbrook Farm, once a sixteenth century manor house. A party of riders on event horses are exercising here, and further down the lane, we are joined by a nice girl on a large chestnut horse with a club foot — he is apparently a superb jumper, although his gait is rather lopsided.

North Marston lies ahead; once a place of pilgrimage. There is a spring with healing properties here, and also a pub with a triangle of grass and picnic tables in front. I have had a sneaking desire to have a pub lunch one day, and this seems to have come at an opportune moment. We take our healing properties from the orange juice and salad sandwiches provided: the horses take theirs on the grass — although bounded by a busy road, neither raise their heads from what must have been a particularly good vintage of pasture!

Some passing drivers do a double take at the sight of two loose horses outside a pub, and a trio of girls come to talk, very envious of our own pilgrimage. A friendly farmer joins in, and gives us a new and apposite phrase to coin: "You've got 'em tied up loose, I see!". A thrush perches on an overhead telegraph pole and provides music with our meal.

On again — but not very far, as we stop to look at North Marston church, unable to resist the attractive gateway. We learn that the roof of the nave, dating from Chaucer's time, was restored by Queen Victoria, making use of money left to her by a local miser. We sign the visitor's book and add the horses' names as well.

A track takes us past Christman Gorse Wood, and then under power lines and pylons in a long grass field.

We amble out along the side of the road to Swanbourne, full of goodwill, good weather, good food, and cocooned against the other world in general. All at once, we are jerked rudely back. A car roars up behind me, ignores my slow down signal and smile, and pulls out as another car comes towards us round the corner. I feel the wind as he passes very close, and fortunately am not in time to warn Jennifer — he literally brushes her saddlebag as he shoots past. If I had shouted, she would have turned — and one more inch might have made a dramatic difference. Jennifer yells furiously after him — he does have the grace to take his foot off the accelerator — but seeing no corpses, continues. Neither of us have the presence of mind to memorise his number.

Thoroughly shaken, we turn off on a quieter lane and continue in silence, following our route alongside a disused railway line. Another short stretch of road, and into fields past several bulls tethered in rows — presumably A.I. bulls, as there are many different breeds. Through a wood next and over another main road. We have begun to notice a curious fact; every major road we approach is full of traffic from both directions —but when we arrive to cross, the Red Sea syndrome occurs — the traffic ceases, and we have a safe passage. Very strange!

We stop for a break by another wood, and for the first time, find we are too hot. The horses too, are restless and don't approve of the grass here, so we are soon under way again.

From Whaddon we have two miles of road to our next bed and breakfast beyond Nash. Here we catch our first sight of the dreaded Milton Keynes, through which we have to ride tomorrow.

Whaddon is a busy place and the road is up with road works. We ignore the diversion signs and pass holes in the ground, diggers and drills, which obligingly stop for us. The diversion rids us of traffic and we have a reasonable, though wearying long haul to Nash. I look back and have a good view of Whaddon church in the evening light, which compensates somewhat for the road.

Our destination reached, and our initial reaction is not favourable. No welcome, long narrow stables, and the horses are unsettled. There is much coming and going of other people, presumably owners or riders of hirelings? Our hay is ready soaked, but tightly stuffed into two blue barrels, which I have to sit astride while Jennifer tugs at the nets to extract them! This should reduce us to giggles, but at the end of the day, we suffer from a slight sense of humour failure!

Jennifer chats up the owner, and we are made to feel more welcome. Things improve; we clean up, get organised and the horses calm down. We have a good ground floor room and shower, and can use the fire escape door to get directly into the yard. The nearest pub is over a mile away, and thankfully we accept a lift. Here we have a large drink, an excellent plate of fish and a first class chocolate pudding, by any standards — and the total bill for two, comes to just over six pounds! Feeling rather full, we walk back to the bed and breakfast, where things have quietened down. Smelly as I am, I can't face the shower. Somehow I have never reached an understanding with these things — I am either scalded, doused in icy water, or drop the soap and slip on the resulting pulp!

Oh for a long, hot bath! And so to bed . . .

Day Nine:
Nash to Castle Ashby

It is an effort to get going this morning, and we feel disinclined to hurry. There is a blacksmith in the yard, and he puts two non-slip nails in Winston's front shoes, which are worn smooth and slipping badly on the road. I am horrified to discover that a set of shoes costs nearly twice as much up here. This blacksmith said he intended to retire and kept putting up his charges to discourage clients, but still they came. Needless to say, he has not yet retired!

Back along the road to Whaddon, and we follow the Swan logo on to a good bridleway, getting ever closer to Milton Keynes. We emerge in the midst of much building work and development. The Swan's Way is well signed on diversionary routes — but we miss the track off the road, as it looks too smart for horses!

A hundred yards further on and we realise that this is indeed the bridleway — a wonderful wood chipping, purpose-built track, running alongside a footpath through pleasantly landscaped parks and gardens. This is the best surface of our entire ride, and we trot on, hardly able to believe we are in the middle of Milton Keynes!

All our fears were unfounded. The needs of riders here are magnificently met — what an example to the rest of the country of what can be achieved.

More surprises in store: we pass under a bridge, and there in front of us, is a herd of black and white plastic cows! The horses stop in astonishment! Not only were the planners hereabouts horse orientated, but someone has a delightfully dotty sense of humour! I wonder what John Betjeman would have thought.

At least three miles of this impressive track takes us out alongside the Grand Union Canal, once a busy link between London and the Midlands. Now it is used for leisure purposes. Winston is wary of a passing barge, and I realise that traffic travelling on water is yet another novelty to him!

We turn off into water meadows and pleasant lakes and ponds. These were previously sand and gravel pits, and are now a nature reserve, full of wildfowl, herons and geese. I suppose all our landscape has evolved over the years by man's manipulation of its resources. I don't know what this place looked like hundreds of years ago, but it is very acceptable in its present form.

We stop for lunch near the ruins of a twelfth century church. The branches of an old thorn tree make a good place to hang our bridles, and as I walk underneath, my hairnet joins them uninvited! The horses' electrolite salts have leached out into my saddle bag, and gone black and gooey over everything. By the time I've emptied my belongings onto the grass, we have created our own tinkers' encampment!

Re-organised again, and a bridge takes the Swan's Way over a waterfall, across a road and up into lovely big fields. We look back from here, over the Ouse Valley, and marvel that we have passed so comfortably through the enormous new city of Milton Keynes.

Leaving a ruined farm on our right, we ride through a nature reserve in a young plantation of woodland. We emerge into the numerous tall stalks of a wireless station, and feel rather like Alice, when she drank the shrinking potion!

The M1 motorway is strangely silent when we reach it; both lanes are blocked and traffic is at a standstill. We ride smugly underneath the bridge on our bridleway. Walking slowly, we go round some cornfields and through and over several good gates and bridges. Looking back, traffic still seems to be frozen on the motorway.

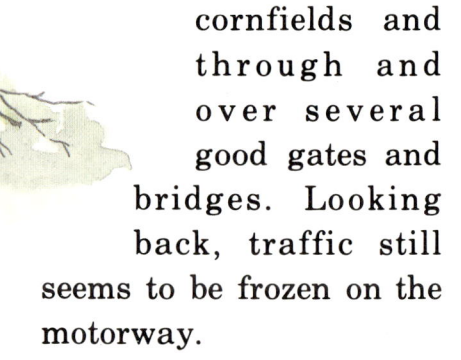

Now we can see our next goal: Salcey Forest lies ahead — vast and green; the source and end of the Swan's Way. It has served us well. From now on, we ride through the forest with the permission of the Forestry Commission's Ranger.

We gain access to the public road through Piddington, and on advice, reluctantly ignore a bridleway which would save us a nasty piece of main road. It is apparently usually blocked, and near the end of the day, we do not want to retrace our steps. We are beginning to regret our late start. It is now evening, and we have some way still to go.

We turn off the main road thankfully, and from this point, are in the capable hands of the agent for Castle Ashby Estate. We have a privately marked route to bring us to his house, where we are to stay the night.

Much privileged, we ride down the wonderful two mile avenue towards Castle Ashby, past a herd of small, dark roe deer, who disappear shyly through the trees at our approach.

We ride in silence. I am very tired and I know Winston is too. How many other weary travellers have ridden this way in the past, to seek sanctuary in the castle walls? Messengers from afar, perhaps, galloping the full length of the avenue to deliver urgent news? As we near the castle, it starts to do a vanishing act, sinking into rising ground, and in the evening light, gives a curiously unreal effect.

We turn away, and dismount to lead the horses the last mile to the Lodge and our penultimate stopping place.

Here Winston and Rose are to have adjoining fields, which will be a welcome treat. Luckily the grass is not too lush, and we turn them loose and carry our kit into one of the lovely arched brick buildings around the yard.

More comfort and wonderful hospitality — and a glorious hot bath! It is *so* hard to stay awake after dinner, and I think I fall asleep during the News!

Once in bed, I dare to wonder, for the first time, whether we will really make it! One more day and seventeen miles to go. Both horses are starting to get sore backs. Both have tired legs. We can only ask for one more day. No more.

Day Ten:
Castle Ashby to Thorpe Malsor

I am still feeling tired when I wake. Both horses seem rather cold and weary, and Winston has not eaten his feed from last night. Should we call a halt now? It is only a couple of hours' trailer ride away . . .

Jennifer joins me, and boosts my flagging morale. The sun comes out and the resident flock of white doves fly up over our heads — and I know now that we will not be defeated.

Breakfast gives us a good start and we are off again. This is the only part of our route where bridleways are an unknown quality. After a mile across fields, our exit is blocked by a stile. We have to make a lengthy diversion to find a way round.

Ahead lies the industrial sprawl of Northampton on our left, and Wellingborough to our right. But between remains a green corridor, and here we plan to pass.

We negotiate a lock over a canal. There is a caravan site here, and I can think of many worse places to live. A charming pack horse bridge takes us over the river Nene, across water meadows into a lane. Here, for a short stretch, we have to watch our feet, for the first time. The black ash surface has patches of broken glass and the odd nail littered around.

We cross the A45 dual carriageway over a bridge, like seasoned old timers, and stop obediently for roadwork traffic lights. Through the village of Ecton, and all at once, I feel at home amongst the warm colour of the ironstone houses.

A quiet lane takes us to Mears Ashby, past Sywell Reservoir and beyond, into and around fields of oil seed rape. Fortunately the flowers have faded, and we do not need to shade our eyes against the raucous yellow. We skirt Sywell Wood and pass through hidden meadows, where it is difficult to realise that we are close to Northampton.

We stop for lunch — tied up loose — in a field by a deserted and spooky farmhouse. It reminds us of Miss Haversham's house in Great Expectations. Tall and overgrown — we half expect to see Pip dart out of the undergrowth!

The bridleway leads us across the middle of a corn field and around several rape fields on hard bumpy headlands. Our route improves with a good bridleway which goes in a straight line for over two miles to Pytchley.

We cross a road and continue on another bridleway to Broughton. Here I have a strange experience of seeing my childhood home, still several miles away, from an entirely new aspect. We pass out of sight through a wood, and a bog, which is probably bottomless in winter, and emerge in the old part of Broughton village.

The road from here on used to be a quiet country lane, where I could ride alone as a small child to have my pony shod at the blacksmiths. The forge is still here, but the road is now a busy one, and we turn off in relief, on the lane that will bring us home within the mile.

I thought we were too tired for further surprises — but suddenly Winston's head goes up, his ears prick, and he starts to stride out eagerly. He has been here for two hunting trips to Leicestershire, but only once has he been on this particular lane. Does he really remember? Is it the sight, or the smell of the place, or some sense that is beyond my comprehension? It is a magical moment after two hundred and fifty miles, and prickles run up my backbone, flooding me with emotion.

In a dream, we meet my mother, waiting to open the gate on to home ground. Rose's head is drooping; she is weary and hasn't caught Winston's mood. How I wish we could tell her that there is only one more field to go!

Past the hovel, into the wood — and in my dazed state, I go the wrong way! At last, we are in the Park now, in front of the house — photographs, bunting over the gate, a large 'Finish' sign — and we are really home. Journey's end at last.

We unpack the horses for the last time, leaving a trail of baggage on the grass, and wandering around in a disconnected sort of way.

This evening, the horses will graze together — clean water, good grass, and peace under the trees at last. Later, both will come in to large airy boxes, and deep beds. There is a possibility of frost tonight, and all comforts await them.

I feel no wild sense of achievement, just low key satisfaction and an enormous appetite! Dozens of scones, cakes, baths and dinner later, and we go quietly out to the stables. Rose is lying flat out, and Winston lying, head droopy.

And so to bed. My window is wide open; an owl hoots outside. I can still hear the refrain in my head, to the tune of Tipperary, that repeated itself to Winston's hoofbeats, on the last stretch of road, when, dismounted, he plodded along behind me:

> *It's a long way to Thorpe Malsor,*
> *It's a long way to go.*
> *It's a long way to Thorpe Malsor —*
> *Because they told me so.*
> *It's long, long journey to Thorpe Malsor,*
> *To the finest Home I know!*

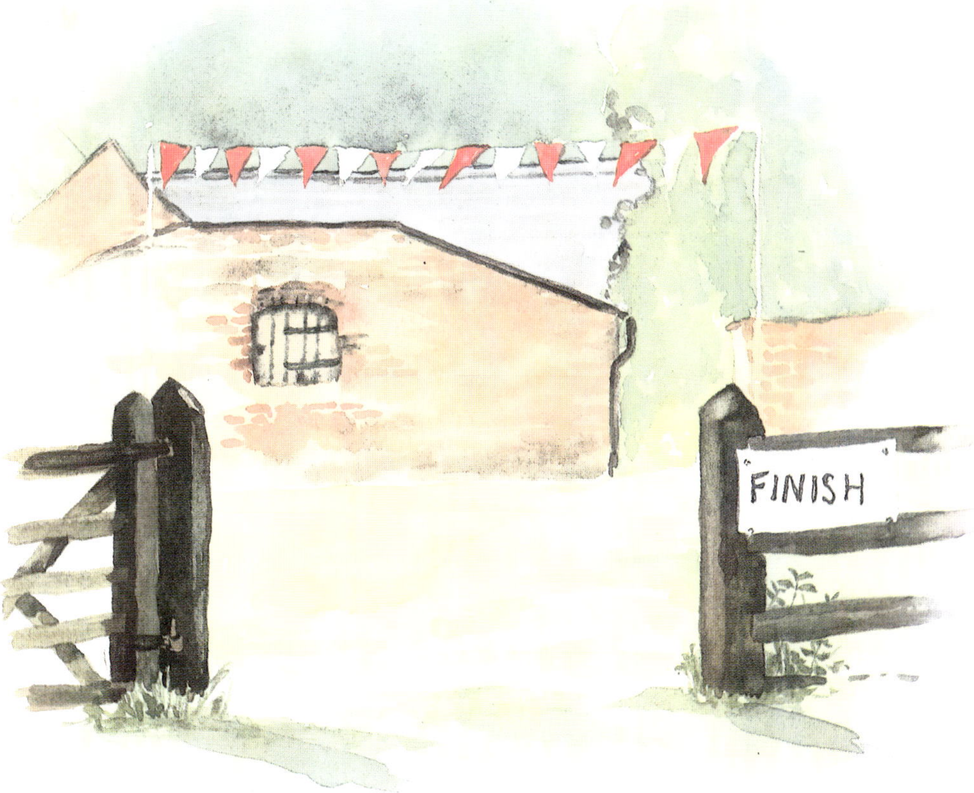
FINISH

Postscript

Waking early has become a habit. The horses finish their breakfast while I remove bandages. Rose knows where she intends to spend the day, and barges out of her stable, heading for the Park, while I am still struggling to do up Winston's headcollar.

They both look well and happy this morning, and I lean on the gate and watch them for a while until they wander out of sight. I drink two cups of tea in the kitchen; resist the temptation — without too much trouble, to start clearing up, and go back to bed.

Warmth and drowsiness return — and also time for retrospection...

For me, a voyage of discovery has ended. I set out, not just on a long distance ride, but to search for something — I knew not what.

We have achieved our main objective — and now it seems so small a thing to do! But as we crossed one range of hills after another, I discovered, to my increasing delight, what it was that I had come to search for.

These days, England seems so ravaged by development, that nothing could manage to remain behind the oft despoiled and battered facade. But we have ridden on green ways, not only through the known unspoilt and beautiful areas, but right up into the very heart of the industrial Midlands. We have covered in excess of two hundred and fifty miles and only sixty were ridden on short stretches of quiet connecting lanes and roads.

My search was for an England that I feared had vanished.

I found instead, a sense of magic in her ancient hills and valleys. I found people leaning on spades in gardens as we passed, who met our eyes and smiled. I found, away from the set, intent faces behind steering wheels, that fellow wayfarers are a happy breed of people. I found a sense of rightness and proportion with the natural way of things — a link with ancient cultures.

I found all this by courtesy of my horse — although I have to say that Winston's aesthetic appreciation of his surroundings, rested entirely on the quality of the grazing available!

Now I know that England is still here, for those who seek her quieter places. It only requires a gentle touch, and the door will open for them to pass through.

Then they will wander the green ways, as we have done, and find great beauty there — behind the land of lost content . . .